THE
CESSATION
OF
LOVE

by Rachel Aston Warren

Warren, Rachel Aston
1st edition.
ISBN: **978-0692575352**
Prolegomenon Publishing

Edited by Jenn Treado
Cover Developed by Nai Obeid
Layout and Design by Isabella Rotman
Author Photo by Erica Silverman
Eye Models: Joseph Ramirez, Nai Obeid, Rachel Aston Warren

Printed and released in Austin, TX

raw_artistry@yahoo.com

"A self-described queer barbie, Rachel Aston Warren (RAW) lives up to this kind of sublimity- that unexpected arrangement of words that catch us off guard and force us to see the beautiful- both as an artist and as a human, which are arguably the same thing. She puts down on page her exploits, reflecting her dynamic understanding of coming of age through navigating the physical and emotional planes of relationships and geography. RAW is queer artistry in a physical form composed of all the things that make us human." ~Jenn Treado

ARTIST'S STATEMENT

I wish to speak individually
And universally

I wish to break people's hearts
And put them back together again

PROLOGUE

DARE

You
Are the game I am playing with myself

MAYBE WE WON'T

Maybe we won't fall in love
Because I don't believe we should fall.
Climb baby
Climb up with me to love and if you fall pick a different mountain not a
different hole.

Love is like quicksand that pulls you up
Quickclouds

Love is like gravity that pulls you from every limb
That opens your stance
That makes you a star.
Let go to the physics of love
Because I want to wish upon you.
For you.

Maybe someday I'll be someone's bomb shelter
Their tornado tunnel
Their crawl space.

Maybe someday somebody will be my bomb
My tornado
My storm

DO THE STARS CHANGE COLOR?

Tree swing, swing tree
Records sing, draw me
Switch walk, swingset hips
Kissing is like test strips

FAVORITE

Your breath in my ear is my favorite song

Your eyes searching my face is my favorite dance

Your sleepy talk my favorite poem

Your last awake squeeze my favorite prayer

Your grinning nod my favorite mantra.

BODY LANGUAGE

My heart is a dancer and my mind is a writer
And my body, my clumsy body
A sculptor?
Sculpting the air with my movements I call dance
Sculpting my words into structures I call poems
Sculpting the love surrounding you
Pushing lightly, stroking the love that rests on your skin to gather in your eyes

My hands cannot help but touch you
It's instinctual, almost a habit now
That does not mean it is done unwillingly
Rather, without thought, or restraint
That is the best way to touch you

My hands cannot help themselves
They cannot help anything but me, and you
Let my hands help me speak
Help me show you how beautiful
A sculpture you are

I've learned on my own kissing is communicating
I knew it, but I was speaking to strangers
Could not understand each other's accents, so only bits and pieces got through
I've learned with you a new language
And now, my dialect is not forced
Our dialogue is not broken
Have we kissed more words than we've spoken?

NAKED, BAKED

Bare foot hiking
Bare legged swinging
Bare bottomed climbing
Bare chested swimming

Bare armed smoking
Bare teethed laughing
Bare watered kissing
Bare bedded fucking

Bare glassed drinking
Bare floored playing
Bare blanketed whispering
Bare lighted confessing

Bare bodied intrigue

FIRST DATE HAIKU

I bought a flower
But you couldn't make it, so
Chrysanthemum dead

THE TEXT I WON'T SEND NOW BECAUSE I'M CONVINCED IT'S INAPPROPRIATE AND I WON'T SEND LATER BECAUSE I'LL FORGET

I had a salad the other day that reminded me of you
I made it
A summer salad:
Baby spinach, cucumber, pear, goat cheese
And pomegranate vinaigrette.
Perfect for the summer.
You and I have always been
Perfect for the summer.
But last year I pulled the wolf
And this one you pirouette, in place
All that face.

Remember this season, in this town?
When we were kids?
Lips, fingertips; stained and puckered with the sap of honeysuckles.
Worried by patches of grass on which to watch the fireworks
And patches of skin we had never shown to anyone.
Holy shit we've grown up since then
And also not.
I found our toys today.
Not your toys
Or my toys
But the ones we bought together.
Isn't it crazy
That when we met, we had no idea
That both of our penises were purple.

My back hurts.
Holy crap does my back hurt.
I know you could help me but I know I won't ask.
Have you ever done yoga in the shower?
Is it bad for you? Have you fallen?
I have
But she doesn't take pictures of me like you used to.
Like you still could.
Like you did with the ice cream cones

Those double-decker adventures
Lemon-blueberry scoops on waffle pyramids
You flavor pharaoh.

You were right.
The cicadas know
All of the secrets of the pond.
All of the skinny dippers think the bullfrogs are bullshit
But I remember ours.
Our secrets and our screams and our plans and our pitfalls.
Remember how we used to not like those vegetables?
Those pits, those palms, those hearts
But you've always been sweeter than the corn.
And I could always relax when I saw that painted smiling cat across the porch
swing
And being barefoot with you wasn't as vulnerable as bare handed
And on Halloween, when I cried over the queen
I think I was crying over you.

And tonight's the solstice
And you return tomorrow
The summer solstice
And it's fucking storming
And you're a storm
The perfect storm.

And anyway
I had a salad
A summer salad
And I thought of you.
For like a second.

NOT A FLOOSY

You asked me
Do you still?

What do you mean darling?
Do I still look at your lips and wish to place a kiss upon them every time you
speak and ask me

Do you still?
Do I still like you, like like you, like the dumb smile on my face likes liking
you ?

Yes.

REASONS WHY

I get really mad at water that doesn't heat up
Fast enough

I guess I was your water
That didn't heat up fast enough

TAKE ME OUT

My love is like the jar of fortune cookies in my kitchen
Overflowing
Collecting for months
Maybe years
A few at the bottom are probably stale.
But the rest are sweet
And filled with words.

FISTBUMPING WITH TREES

Right on cue, echoing my conscience:
"What are you thinking about?"

You, good sir
Your hands, good sir
The space of skin between the corners of your mouth and your bottom
eyelashes, good sir.
That's where your smile starts
It ends with your teeth on your lower soft-edge lip
Your smile is strong, for it lifts hearts, eyes, other smiles.
What do I know about you but your walk?
Feet more gentle than hip bones
Hip bones, at my rib-level.
Hip bones more gentle than prayer beads
Prayer beads, in my mouth.
In the catacombs, surrounded by girls
Shy girls. Scared girls. Straight girls?
I feel your eyes behind me; the stone wall behind them
And I can't stop thinking about hate crimes.

Right on cue, bouncing off my conscience:
"What are you thinking about?"

You, teacher
Your hair, teacher
The goddess on your wall, your arm, your heart, teacher.
What do I know about you but your words?
The words we've exchanged in ratio to all we've thought
About each other
About each other
They're just the tip of the iceberg.
Once you pointed out the woodpeckers; it's all I hear
Like a drumroll; a toy train approaching; a knock-knock rap
Trying to get at my brain, to decode my heart.

Right on cue, waltzing with my conscience:
"What are you thinking about?"

You, player
Your eyes, player
Getting high, and staying high, and self-sabotage, player.
Eyes as keys, as locks, lost
Simultaneously sluts and monks
Binging and purging our desires
Could you be loved?
What do I know about you but your name?
Peace, calmness, bliss
Indeed.
Our words on pointe
Doing ballets across eggshells
Speaking in sign-language song.

Right on cue, mimicking my conscience:
"What are you thinking about?"

…………………..Nothing.

"Good. That's what I like to hear."

REPEAT

Touch me
Touch me
Touch me, please
But don't know me
Don't know me
Please, don't know me

THE ART OF LESBIAN LAYOVERS

I was lying naked in bed, legs wrapped around a pillow
Scrolling through her Tumblr, and I thought,

"Oh shit"

She's getting over someone too; too much?; last week; now?
Right now.

I am happy for her heart to have loved like the wind
But grieve for her pain, as if I don't have the same

We could get over them together
Use each other as stunt doubles through winter's obstacle course
Create a playground, fall down, get pushed, scraped up, lick each others'
wounds, make love.

But will we ever get promoted
From substitute teachers
To full-time muse?

LINCHPIN

Everyone envies
The life of a housecat
Free food
Naps in the sun
And most importantly
Unmistakable love.

You know you've said it before
"That cat's got life figured out"
Remember that
The next time you're considering
Putting anything above
Love.

LEGEND

It kind of strikes me when you say I don't know you
In earnest or in jest
Because I want to.

Your mind is not a book
It has no Table of Contents for me to run my finger down and skip to a
numbered page
It has no beginning or end
I don't want to read it
Your mind is land and sea and sky
And I am an eager cartographer
If I were a kindergarten class what would you bring me for show and tell?

You are not mine
I do not have any part of you
Except parts of your time
And hopefully
Eternally
Parts of your heart.

I don't know you
Because your past is not a childhood movie I can quote without reminder
I do not know every detail of your nurture
But I am slowly absorbing your nature
And the past is not the first thing I want to know about you
I want to know your present more than anything
And hopefully
Later
I can know your future.

REASONS WHY #2

It got cold when you left the room
And the rain finally smelled sweet to me

LOVE ME NOW

I want you to talk to me
There's never a day that I don't
Even ones like today, when I can't smile
I want you to talk to me

I want you to touch me
All of the time
I want your eyes to light up when I come in the room
I want you to not be able to do anything else until you hug me

I want you to flirt with me
At work and at home
I want you to lust after my laugh
And always watch me walk away

Never stop burning the grilled cheese because I'm bending over looking in the
fridge
Never stop racing the clock because you have to just get one more lick in
Never stop smoking over my shoulder because you don't want to let go
Never stop dopily interrupting me because you need to kiss me,
Kiss me,
Kiss me hard

FULL MOON HAIKU

I watch you watch her
And I wish, for you and I
Cessation of love

GOOD LYER

It's as if we're both lying in a bed
Pretending to be asleep.
I adjust my breathing
To sound like sleeping.
You adjust your shifting
To feel like dreaming.
I'm pretty good at it now
So you believe I'm slumbering.
But you
Suppose you really could be
I actually can't tell.

LONESTAR

This is why I don't drink, she says, holding her hand to her stomach, holding a
break in her heart
She doesn't make eye contact for the whole morning
She can't think of any reason to look up.

This is why I don't drink, she says, thinking of her legs, the head between them,
how she can't feel any oral passion
I still love you when you're drunk
But
I do not love it when you drink.

This is why I don't drink, because you can get out of bed and take a shower and
I can be hurt you didn't ask me to join
She thinks, how ridiculous: this over hang-up on every word.

This is why I don't drink, she slams her knee into the bed corner, again; slams
her jaw closed tight.

Do I love you? How much do I love you? In a measurement of how many
times I've cried all the way home from your house, today: four times much

This is why I don't drink, because I had fun but I still wish we didn't
Because I can wake up and realize
This is the beginning of the decline.

THE LOVERS

And after all this time
We're still not friends

OCEANS

There have been poems written about my eyes
There have been poems written about my eyes that I've never seen
There's a poem, written in French, about my eyes

But here's mine

Tell me, at what point did you look into my eyes
And stop seeing oceans?

SLIDE AFFECTS

Your slightly minty goodbye kiss
Not the first to be rushed, hurried;
Like a mis-placed comma, lost somewhere in the sentence of the morning.
Your slightly minty goodbye kiss
Not the last to be had, hiding, disconnected
From the goings on in and around it.

We are not good for each other
And I don't know if we ever were.
We were there, we were alive, and we smiled-
I suppose those are good.
But I don't know if you realize it now
We cannot carry this anymore.

I spent the whole car-ride thinking of my answer to a question you did not ask.
Well, you see
I wanted to press my fingers to my throat
And you saw something in the corner
And all I could do was breathe
And all you could do was break
Putting figurines in the doorway of the room with the backwards lightswitch.

Me, no; but you scared yourself.
The day after I went off you fell in.
I hear words again, however faint
And you see blobs of dark geometry-
Biology, maybe
Chemistry, baby.

With your lightly minted au revoir kiss
Fare, well, Love
Take care of yourself.

RED

Every car I've owned
Or driven for an extended period of time
Has died.
Once a quick but unexpected end
Mostly a slow, rusty, screeching, painful death.

It's probably my fault
I don't know shit about oil changes and brake checks
Re-alignment and snow tires and engine lights.

I wore my seatbelt with you.
But I guess I should have learned how to open the sunroof
Would owning a manual make a difference?

All of these funerals won't stop me from buying another in the future
Just because I knew how to drive you
Doesn't mean I knew how to take care of you.

I LOVE YOU MORE THAN FOOD

The only thing I've done every single day of my life
Is eat.
So when I tell you that I love you more than food
You better fucking believe I'm serious.

FOOTNOTES

I have an invisible bruise on my foot
It is deep but only hurts with the right pressure[1]
I suppose I have an invisible bruise on my heart
I haven't found it yet
Nor do I know exactly what pressure makes it hurt[2]

My heart is the snooze button
My heart is the blanket I wake up to find on the floor
My heart is the line of pillows I use to replace you when I sleep alone
My heart is the check I write that always bounces[3]

My heart is a drunk driver
Getting behind the wheel before it's ready
Saying "FUCK IT" and having to unsoberly deal with the consequences
My heart is a partier but is not able to host the party[4]

My heart might be past its expiration date
I want to wash my heart out with soap[5]
Push 1 of epi, use the paddles and if my heart restarts[6]
I'll be myself again

My heart is a goldfish[7]
My heart is the one I glance at when something on the tv strikes me funny
If my heart could get diagnosed I reckon it'd have congenital analgesia

My heart isn't in the game[8]
My heart is the spectator who avoids the shows with audience participation

---

[1] I have no idea how I got it
[2] Therefore I don't know how to avoid it
[3] *Insufficient funds*
[4] It may be hungover
[5] Make it stand with its nose in the corner
[6] -When it restarts-
[7] A 3 second memory span
[8] It's the referee

My heart, all it has on its mind is walls
Great Wall of China, Berlin Wall[9]

My heart is the disconnected phone line
The number of which I will always have memorized
My heart is the empty plot of land where one of my homes once stood
I live in a different home now but not on that land
That home only exists in our memories[10]

My heart is the collection of bookmarks I have
Too many for the amount of books I could hold my place in at once[11]
My heart is the unexplainable lump in my throat
My heart is the reason I use pencils instead of pens
My heart is just working on its gen eds

When bears are in hibernation, do they dream?
My heart isn't hibernating, but is the cave where hibernation occurs
Will you choose my heart to hibernate in for awhile?
Past the winter[12]

My heart is an itch I didn't know I had until I scratched it
My heart is the powerful scent of my hair
Enveloping me after being up and away from my face

My heart is a beach
Each microscopic pebble of sand a crack[13]
You are the tide, the waves
You come and go, refreshing my stones
A beach, so beautiful from far away
But up close, without water, those grains can scratch you, can scorch you

---

[9] Whatever the fuck Humpty Dumpty sat on
[10] That land tells no stories
[11] But there just in case
[12] And then past that
[13] A heartbreak

My heart is an hourglass?
Of course it is, but can you be there too
A typical hourglass is made with dry sand
But let mine contain a beach!

My heart is a game of Red Rover[14]
Run at me with all your force and try to break through my heart
If you succeed you'll be on my side
Part of my chain of people, of memories, of loves
If you can't get through just yet
Retreat and when it's my turn
I'll just send you right over again

My heart is the song I have stuck in my head that I never knew the words to
My heart is an organ
Sometimes the kind with pipes, big and small, loud and soft, triumphant and sinister
But most of the time the kind with blood vessels and arteries and tissues
My heart is just thoughts[15]

---

[14] Red Rover, Red Rover, send her right over
[15] My thoughts are just chemicals

SIMPLY HAIKU

You told me love is
Simple, but then you went and
Complicated it

BUFF PRINCESS

We texted all night
About gender roles in theatre, and memories of last winter,
About missing our mania

Later on I couldn't sleep-
Started thinking about that ghost you saw in our bedroom,
Wondering if it's still there-
Or if it was just me haunting you

BIAS

You asked me how I see you.

I see a human, two feet, turned slightly in, never on the ground for too long.
Legs strong and determined, your walk is eager, the backs of your knees push
away what you're leaving behind, all the negativity behind you.

Hips bruised and happy
Waist hidden, but there, shoulders calm and modest
The body of a deity.

Now your face
Your face is a dream.
A dream I can hold in my hands, soft
A lion, kitten, deer, bear.

When the corners of your mouth move toward your temples
Like a drawstring curtain on a glowing stage
The world turns on all of the lamps, bulbs, speakers, sounds
Everything in my heart is in high definition surround sound
And outside is beautiful muffled fuzz.

BRUNCH

He holds his fork vertically so the tongs cover one of his eyes. "It looks like you're in jail," he says.

She bugs her eyes, "Help!" she says.

He giggles, closes the eye with no fork in front of it, and tells her, "Do that again." She does. "Now, move your hands in a bit," he says. She does. "A bit more. Oh, there we go. Do it again."

She smiles, then, holding her fists as if holding bars of a cell, says, "Let me out, let me out!"

He drops his fork to his plate, laughing with squinted eyes.

"I love you."

WHAT I'M THINKING WHEN I'M STARING

You're so beautiful; but you don't believe it
I tell you you are; you say 'no' and you mean it
And yes, I mean your face, your flawless face; and your body.

Who-so-ever made you think otherwise?
Made you believe this beauty-less lie?
It can't have been your Parents, since you're half of them each
They're beautiful, too, and we see them in you.

Was it The Mirror? Tricky mirror; stained with society?
I told it to stop reminding you of untruths; uncouth, sticky mirror

It must have been a stranger; or strange strange deniers
It must have been someone who's never seen you in the morning; sunlight so
bright on your pink cheekbones; triceps, tops of your feet stretching reaching
for love.

Or was it you? Stubborn you, a-little-mixed-up you
Ears so beautiful they're blind; mouth so beautiful it's deaf
Almond grizzly avocado skin eyes, so so beautiful
They squint and close as you laugh at yourself; and say 'no'...

It must be because you've never seen you laugh at yourself
It must be because you've never seen the look of surprise
On your face
When I tell you

SLEEPTALKING TO A SAINT

They kissed me on The Tender Spot
Right on the neck.
It woke me up
'It itches' I said
I whined, writhed with pain
'Don't scratch it' they said.
I awoke again
They put lotion on all of my spots.
A helpless leper in the night
In and out of consciousness, ever conscious of their presence, alert, awake,
helpful
Putting me first, my prayers of pain
As if washing my feet, the prophet.

AND THEN, AGAIN

Can I imagine my life with you?

Can I imagine walking the dog around the block, right before it starts to rain?

Can I imagine making breakfasts, snacks, and dinner with you, for you?

Can I imagine sitting, breathing, watching you put your bike together in our living room?
You put your foot on the handle, the handle on the ground, to stabilize the frame
Line up the axle and insert the wheel
Grab the wrench from the coffee table and-

OH NO! The bike is tipping ove-

You catch it before it makes a sound
Tighten the bolt, and give the wheel a spin
Done.
You flip it over and spin the opposite one
You set it down, carefully, laying it along the theatre seats

I ask, "Do you enjoy this?"
You say, "Yeah. I do. It's relaxing."

SHE'S GOT THAT POWER

Her solicitude belongs in an enchanted forest
Surrounded by helpful squirrels and birds
She interrupts herself to pick up trash on the side of the path
And I feel as defended as the ground she walks on

My eyes gaze upon hers, curious blue planets
Her lips, lovely wet pillows, I kiss
I kiss between her breasts, her scent is a gift
She puts her finger in her mouth, as I sink between her legs

Her beauty belongs on the Titanic
As the leading lady, the love interest, the loquacious lustful lynx
She drapes her silky self across the velvet furniture
And I'm sunk

KNOW BY HEART

I have love to give.
To wrap up in printed paper and bows
Or to set candidly on your table.
I have love to leave
Moistened on your forehead
And certain in your eyes.

I would deliver it simply
I would give it passionately
I would leave it riddle-lessly.
I want to shower you with love
I want to feed and sip you love
I want to tuck you into love.

I have love to expose.
To exhibit gracefully, sometimes
And later in unrestrained display.
I have love to tell
To drunkenly yell
And hoarsely whisper.

I would not censor myself
I would be honest with them
I would not make you dig.
I want to inspire love in you
I want to listen to your love
I want to lend you love.

I have love to recycle.
To use your leftovers
And build something tastier.
I have love to plant
To trust it to grow on its own
And to cultivate when you need.

I want to get lost in love with you
I want to float on love with you

I want to take love hikes with you.
I want to walk to the pace of love
I want to watch love with you
I want to mix, spice, and bake love alongside you.

I have carefully mapped words for you
And I have unedited scrawls
Of love
For you
I would plop them in your mailbox
And hide them in your books
And lose them in your couch.

I want to read to you love
I want to sing to you love
I want to dance love with you.

GEOMETRY LESSON

In the shower fucking your pelvic bone with my quadricep
One arm is parallel with the wall and one knee is the rightest angle there ever
was
[Against the door, my mons Venus right above your hip bone
{Making every angle of the couch acute}]

You fucked my mind when you read me yours
You fucked my body when your eyes got me wet (and your smile can make me
orgasm)
You made love to my heart when outside it was -10• and my bed was a sauna
and we played Rack-O in our underwear and I forgot to be hungry and we slept
on the couch until 6 AM

The third day we had sex was Epiphany
The three stars on your cheek are making fun of me for falling
So I kiss the Holy Trinity one by one and thank them all for leading me to you

Your skin smelled like holy water
My life is dehydrated
I could drink only you for all the days
But baby ration yourself
Because everybody needs it
And nobody is getting enough

I don't need to ask if you consider yourself an optimist
Your soul emanates joy and your smile: vision
I don't need to ask if you think asymmetry is beautiful
Because if you said no I know you'd have the best reason to back it up
I don't need to ask what your biggest fear is
Because I know whatever you're scared of won't scare me away

I've never been afraid of heights
Just my ears can't take the pressure
But I will celebrate the popping
And make a fanfare on my drums
If it means I keep falling

I've been up above for awhile
He said we had chemistry the day we went to the humane society for fun and I
had no make-up on
She got offended when we were laughing I said we were like sisters
They helped me into a corset and thought I was a sex goddess and told their
fathers they had a girlfriend
But I never wrote the poem

This is for you
So you know when I knew
When we exchanged our favorite Andrea Gibson lines
The way you got so excited that Balkan Beat Box was playing
This is for you
I'm writing the poem
That's how I know
I've been writing it since I really looked into your eyes
As earth tone as you can get, your eyes
Like the wisest river and the ripest tree, your eyes
This is for you
So you know that I know
I know, baby
I know, human
I know, love

I'm gayer than poetry
And life itself
If "queer" was the clue for 3 Down in my heart
I'd fill you in
And if I was flipped in a game of memory
You'd be my match

You put me in a haze
Like the fog penetrating the Halifax bay
You are the lighthouse with the glow of lanterns and candles
(When laying with you is mutual meditation)
I raise the white flag of the under flesh of my arms
As you glue them to the floor

I could look back into my treasure chest of words I wrote for other people
when my heart hadn't met you yet
Sift for the good ones, polish them, scrap the rest
Anything lovely I've written for any other lover
Would be truer now for you than when I wrote it

I wish I had written those poems for you instead of them
But wishes are for clocks and eyelashes
Like the one you pulled off my face not knowing you yourself had two under
your left eye
And I blew on your fingertip so instinctively I forgot to make a wish
Because I was already holding you

I wonder if you believe in luck
Because that day you brought me curry
I found a penny on the ground that was so dirty I couldn't tell if it was tails or
heads
So I decided it meant I should make my own luck and give you head

My head is too fast for my lips
My brain is in a long-distance relationship with my lips
All my lips want is to be close to you
And all my brain wants is for my lips to form words that will make you stay

I wonder what you'll say

I wonder how many poems have dared to document you
I wonder how many portraits have claimed to capture you
I wonder how many songs think that they know you

Coming soon...

February 4th, 2016;

RAW
Poetry and Prose for the Queer, Sentient Being

May 4th, 2016

Humans: A Study

Special Thanks to Jenn Treado for being the most supportive and talented editor, and wise friend; to Nai Obeid for blowing my mind with brilliant badassery; to Maura Kinney for hearing me talk about love for almost a decade; to Lindsey Lee for shaping me into the person I've always wanted to be; to Erica Silverman for being my artistic angel; to Isabella Rotman for being a magical presence, and so generous; to Joseph Ramirez for inspiration and encouragement; to Timothy Miles for musical genius and positive vibes always; and to Emily Warren for being my person. I love you all.

Currently residing in her birth state of Texas, Rachel and her cat, Garcia, live in a fairytale flat in Austin that is frequented and adored by friends and lovers alike.

RAW dabbles in all things aesthetic: writing (poetry, prose and theatre), the stages of burlesque and modeling, and has been known to pick up the camera from time to time.

www.ingramcontent.com/pod-product-compliance
Lightning Source LLC
Chambersburg PA
CBHW070038070426
42449CB00012BA/3087